THE SINGLE
SHOULD BRITAIN JOIN?

'No more distressing moment can ever face a British government than that which requires it to come to a hard, fast and specific decision.'

Barbara W. Tuchman

The Single Currency:
Should Britain Join?

A *Guardian* Debate

Martin Kettle
John Palmer
Larry Elliott
Victor Keegan

VINTAGE

Published by Vintage 1997

2 4 6 8 10 9 7 5 3 1

First published in Great Britain by
Vintage, 1997

Vintage
Random House, 20 Vauxhall Bridge Road, London SW1V 2SA

Random House Australia (Pty) Limited
20 Alfred Street, Milsons Point, Sydney,
New South Wales 2061, Australia

Random House New Zealand Limited
18 Poland Road, Glenfield,
Auckland 10, New Zealand

Random House South Africa (Pty) Limited
Endulini, 5A Jubilee Road, Parktown 2193, South Africa

Random House UK Limited Reg. No. 954009

A CIP catalogue record for this book
is available from the British Library

ISBN 0099773511

Papers used by Random House UK Ltd are natural, recyclable
products made from wood grown in sustainable forests. The
manufacturing processes conform to the environmental
regulations of the country of origin

Set in 10½/12 Sabon by SX Composing DTP, Rayleigh, Essex
Printed and bound in Great Britain by
Cox & Wyman, Reading, Berkshire

A VINTAGE ORIGINAL

CONTENTS

AN INTRODUCTION

MARTIN KETTLE

BEFORE THE END of 1997 the fifteen member states of the European Union (EU) will meet to make the final decision about whether to create a single European currency in 1999, first by locking their exchange rates together, as required by the Treaty of Maastricht, and then by proceeding to replace their national currencies with a single currency, which can be traded with the same value from Lapland to Lisbon and from Donegal almost to the gates of Istanbul.

At that point, and perhaps even sooner, the British government must also decide whether it will join this historic economic and political project. If the single currency goes ahead and Britain joins it, the pound sterling will cease to exist from the start of 2002 and will be replaced by a new form of currency, known as the Euro. The British government – like all the other member governments of the EU – will necessarily lose many of the powers over domestic monetary policy which, in theory at least, national governments still possess today. In return, supporters of the single currency argue, Britain and Europe will enjoy long-term economic stability, will complete the abolition of barriers to a single European market and will bring to an end the periodic currency crises which, particularly in Britain's case, have for decades afflicted governments and individuals. With a single currency, moreover, the integration of Europe will have taken a massive, and not the last, step forward.

Alternatively, the British government may decide to invoke the opt-out from the single currency, negotiated by John

Major at Maastricht in 1991. But in that case it will have to make clear whether it regards the opt-out as temporary or permanent. Will it 'watch and wait', observing the single currency from within an outer band of the EU, preserving the option of joining it later (perhaps with others) in a second or subsequent phase? Or will it turn its back more decisively on the Europe of the single currency – and perhaps ultimately on the EU itself – and go it alone as a wholly sovereign state within Europe, as Switzerland and Norway are trying to do?

Whatever the outcome, it will undoubtedly be a historic decision for Britain and must involve the most careful and responsible estimate of the foreseeable consequences of such a change. Clearly no nation will commit itself to the single currency unless it expects to gain a combination of political and economic benefits. But the precise nature of these benefits differs in each nation's case, and they must be set against the political and economic costs that will also result from the new currency.

To embark upon a single currency or not to embark? To join or not to join? These connected questions pose the single greatest dilemma facing Europe since at least the collapse of Communism, and perhaps since the end of the last European war in 1945. Yet the decisions will mainly be made, not by the citizens of Europe acting as Europeans, but by the citizens of the individual nations – and in most cases not by them, but by their governments, acting on their behalf. Whatever decisions are reached, they are therefore national decisions, in which each nation will determine, for its own distinct reasons, whether this change is for them or not.

For Britain, and to a greater or lesser extent for every other EU nation too, it is a decision that brings many other questions to a head. Does Britain now accept that its national interest – and, even more grandly, its destiny – lies in full economic union with the continent of Europe? Or does it have some other vision of its international role? If so, what is that alternative role? Are the British people prepared to see other Europeans (and in particular the Germans, against whom their forebears fought two world wars in the first half of this century) as comrades, rather than rivals? Will we accept the continuing redefinition, and even replacement, of our own financial, legal and parliamentary institutions within a European framework? And, to put the question of European monetary union at its crudest: are we happy to abolish the pound?

The European question, or one of the many variations upon it, has dominated British political life since at least the 1950s. Nearly a quarter of a century ago, after much initial hesitation and following a humiliating earlier rebuff from General de Gaulle, Britain finally joined the original six founding nations in the European Economic Community (EEC). In 1975 that decision was confirmed by a majority of two to one in what is still the only national referendum ever to have been held in the United Kingdom. Yet the referendum did not finally settle the matter, as it was intended to (a relevant point for all advocates of referendums). After a lull in the late 1970s and early 1980s, Europe began to re-emerge as an unresolved issue in British public life. For the past ten years, as other conflicts have been at least temporarily reconciled, Europe has provided the greatest fault-line in our politics, and today it shows no sign whatsoever of losing its power to divide.

Only someone with no sense of history could imagine that this is a simple decision for any nation, and especially for an island nation like ours – one of the most durable and globally influential states from this part of the world, whose whole story is shot through with the consequences of its relationships with the peoples of continental Europe. At the same time, only someone with great arrogance of vision could imagine that the decision about joining the single European currency will form the final chapter of this long national saga – or, indeed, of any of Europe's other sagas.

Yet that is not in any way to diminish the significance of the decisions that will be taken in 1997. Rather, it underlines the momentous nature of the hour in which our generation of Britons and Europeans now live. At a time when politicians and the media are both treated with contempt by many in our society, we need to rescue the European debate from hysteria, trivia, half-truth, obfuscation and nonsense. Recognising the importance of the issues and the need for clarity in an often

3

technical and obscure debate, we need to assess with care and thoroughness the greatest of all public decisions now standing before the British people.

What follows is an attempt by four colleagues at the *Guardian* newspaper to debate the problem – intelligently, honestly and, we hope, entertainingly – and lead to a conclusion that the British people are invited to follow. At the end of the day, Britain will have to make a decision one way or the other, just as the respective contributors to this short study have done. But as this introduction has tried to make clear, deciding whether or not to join the single currency is not straightforward. It is not as simple a calculation as seeing whether the price of the same pair of shoes is better in one shop than another. Nor should we overdramatise it. The single currency is not one of the great existential dilemmas of all time, though it *is* perhaps the most important political decision to be taken in the lifetime of many people alive today. But whatever decisions are eventually made at the end of 1997, Britain and Europe will still be coexisting, long after the current debate has vanished on the wind.

BACKGROUND TO THE DEBATE
MARTIN KETTLE

MONETARY UNION IS an economic question. But no monetary union – and certainly not this one – was ever begun except for political reasons. In monetary union, economics and politics are inescapably intertwined. Historically, the reason for this is very simple. Rulers and governments have always wanted to control the amount and value of the money in circulation in their lands. So the idea that monetary union can be a purely economic decision unsullied by mere politics is complete idealism. We must therefore beware at the outset any attempt to persuade us that the decision to enter a single currency is 'purely' an economic decision, or 'purely' a political one.

It is also important to recognise a point that has now become somewhat overlooked in the post-Maastricht debate. A single currency is not the inevitable outcome of monetary union. A form of monetary union could be achieved without a single currency, inasmuch as different nations or banking areas can decide to lock their exchange rates together, on some predetermined basis and according to rules which mean, in effect, that they function as one. The European Monetary System, whose exchange-rate mechanism (ERM) Britain joined in 1990 and then left so precipitately in 1992, is one such example. So, in the 1920s was the International Gold Standard, in which the value of each currency was set in terms of a fixed value in gold. The fact that these models have now been abandoned by the signatories of the Maastricht Treaty does not mean that they are outmoded or irrelevant as possible alternatives to a single currency.

Probably the most influential precedent of monetary union in modern European history was inescapably politically motivated, and it is surprising how infrequently this is referred to by those who try to explain why the current debate takes the course it does. This precedent was the creation of a single German currency during the late nineteenth and early twentieth centuries. It was a relevant and significant event for today's European argument for two reasons: first, because unlike the Gold Standard or the ERM, it worked; second, because it worked in Germany, the most powerful and important country in Europe, and the one that is now the driving force behind moves towards a single European currency. For it is neither a 'pro-German' nor an 'anti-German' observation to say that the single currency would not be on the agenda, were it not for Germany. This is simply a statement of fact and a recognition of the dynamic reality of modern Europe.

The creation of the single German currency contains certain parallels with the situation in the EU today. Early nineteenth-century Germany was a patchwork of independent and semi-independent states, many with their own currencies. Their potential economic and political strength was far greater than their actual fragmented strengths. In 1834 an attempt was made to bring the economies of the German states together by the creation of a customs union, the Zollverein, based on fixed exchange rates creating a single German market. It was a decision that suited the manufacturers and traders of the German states, but it enjoyed popular support, too. The single market, in other words, preceded the political union of Germany in 1871, although this in turn preceded the creation of a single German currency, which was not finally achieved until 1909.

Germany's nineteenth-century experience is therefore not a precise forerunner of European integration. The sequence experienced in Germany – customs union followed by political union and only then by monetary union – is in fact significantly different from the sequence that appears to be taking shape in modern Europe – customs union followed by monetary union, and then perhaps by political union. And there is no iron law that dictates that customs union necessarily leads to a particular outcome. What is clear is that, at least in a German context, customs union by itself is seen as a precedent for further union of some sort. There is no doubt that this assumption underpins most German thinking about the EU today, and that it is one of the principal reasons why Germany is so committed to a monetary union that otherwise entails serious economic, and perhaps political, sacrifices for its own citizens and may even risk jeopardising the economic and political stability that is the great achievement of the German nation over the past half-century.

Yet if a passion for logic and completeness was the only motive behind European monetary union (EMU), there would be no need to take the project seriously. An international monetary system would have its advocates, in the same way that there are advocates of a common international language or of world government – the Euro would be to economics what Esperanto is to politics.

The reason why European monetary union is taken more seriously than Esperanto is because the postwar history of so many European nations has gradually made it a logical and realisable goal for an aggregation of otherwise conflicting national interests. The explanation for this lies deeply embedded in the experience of the peoples of Europe in two world wars. European union is not, save for a few misty-eyed idealists, a project with an enormously long history. This is not to say that there have not been earlier attempts to unify Europe. There have, but they have taken very much more coercive and destabilising forms than anything that has been discussed in our time. From the Roman Empire to the Third Reich, previous pan-European projects have tended to be based on force of arms rather than on persuasion. The hegemonic projects of Charlemagne and of Charles V were based on the power of the Christian Church; the Napoleonic Empire was the child of the French Revolution; and the international Communist movement (in many ways the least belligerent of all the pre-1989 European unification projects) was likewise the offspring of the Russian Revolution. Until recent decades Europeanisation has meant military conquest.

The Europeanisation movement that grew up in post-1945 Europe was different. It was not an offensive movement, seeking to annexe territories in defiance of their peoples (or at least their governments); initially at least, it was entirely defensive. It was the offspring of political and social experiences of the most searing kind, which many people in Britain, having experienced the crisis of 1939-45 in a more heroic mode, innocently – but disastrously – fail to understand to this day. In Germany, the European project was a reaction against the nationalism and militarism of the Third Reich, while in France (and to some extent also in Germany) it was a revolt against the experience of three Franco-German wars within seventy years. But it was also based on a more positive belief, characteristic of the immediate post-1945 era, that economic planning was a natural route to efficiency and growth. In particular, there was a common agreement in France and Germany that starvation of the people (a direct experience in 1945 for both countries, especially Germany) could be avoided by means of planned and coordinated agricultural subventions, as well as a belief that industrial rebuilding (all three wars had been waged in the then prosperous French coalfields and steel belt) should be coordinated, rather than competitive.

The Franco-German alliance that has dominated postwar western Europe was a response to this situation and has been the cornerstone of all Europeanisation ever since. Without these two nations acting in concert, there would be no Europeanisation project. With them acting together, no other European nation can easily resist being dragged along in their slipstream. That remains as true today, in the context of the monetary union debate, as it has always been.

Yet the nature of the European project that emerged between 1945 and 1989 was fundamentally different from the one that exists today. The EU evolved as a result of, and in the context of, the Cold War. It was a union that provided benefits and security to member states (notably France and

Italy) with electorally significant Communist parties. As time passed, it increasingly acquired superpower aspirations of its own, asserting its claim to be treated as a third force in world affairs, in the front line against the Soviet Union, but distinct from the United States. With the US deployment of Cruise missiles in Europe in the early 1980s, these claims began to have genuine popular resonance. They were particularly welcome to France – for most of the 1980s, the only social democratic government in any of the advanced industrial powers. And it is no accident that a French politician of the Left was decisive in making the push towards integration. No single event did more to popularise the idea of European union than the Cruise missile crisis, and no single person did more to create the conditions in which it could be achieved than Jacques Delors during his period as President of the European Commission, which began in 1985.

If Communism had not collapsed, then the Europe that Delors planned would almost certainly have been achieved with far less trepidation than surrounds it today. But Communism did collapse – peacefully for the most part, and at sometimes dizzying speed, between 1989 and 1991. The result was the removal of much of the international context of the EU's existence and, in particular, of the surrounding justifications being offered for the various schemes of unification in vogue at the time. After 1991 the EU no longer stood as a third force between the two superpowers. Indeed, its largest member state, Germany, was transformed and preoccupied by the addition of the former Communist DDR and by a reunification based from the start on a strong single German currency, whatever the social consequences.

At a stroke, or very nearly, the case for European unification was fundamentally transformed. Instead of being an essentially consolidatory project between market economies in a divided Europe (as it had been until 1989-91), it now rapidly became more ambitious, and in some respects politically more idealistic, with the extension of these aims to embrace the former Communist states. Now that there was no separate justification for a unified western Europe, the advocates of unification reached out to embrace central and eastern Europe, though invariably the member states had very different reasons for doing so. Britain, pragmatic and insular on most other issues, became a fervent ideological advocate of expansion. Germany, already ideologically disposed towards Europeanisation, now became an advocate of their inclusion, because its own inescapable geographical considerations compelled this. Of the big member states, only France – concerned above all to stick close to Germany – was able to adjust to the collapse of the Berlin Wall without a grinding of political gears and a redefinition of political goals.

The upshot was the Maastricht conference of December 1991, which produced a treaty conceived in the old Europe but delivered in the new. The treaty set the terms of the present debate about monetary union. It was designed, according to its first clause, to create 'an ever-closer union among the peoples of Europe' – an intentionally ambiguous formulation originally set out in the Treaty of Rome, but here given flesh by the other articles agreed at Maastricht, which completed the European single market and extended the harmonisation process to cover aspects of foreign, internal and economic policies.

Maastricht laid down an 'irreversible' path to economic and monetary union of the member states, with the creation of a single currency by 1 January 1999. It made provision for the creation of an independent European Central Bank governed by an executive board of six people, linked to a network of national central banks, and with the sole right to authorise the issue of banknotes within the EU. It established the principle of coordination in national economic policies and set out the 'convergence criteria' that must be met by member states before they could switch to a single European currency.

The treaty also set out four general goals for convergence: price stability; low budgetary deficits; stable exchange rates; and acceptable long-term interest rates. These were given specific form in a separate protocol to the treaty, which stated that:

- inflation, as measured by the consumer prices index,

must not be more than 1.5 per cent higher than the average of the three best-performing member countries;

- budgetary deficits must be less than 3 per cent of a nation's gross domestic product (GDP);
- exchange rates must not have been devalued or have fluctuated by more than 4.5 per cent within the European exchange-rate mechanism;
- long-term interest rates must be within 2 per cent of the average of the lowest three member countries.

The treaty required the member states to meet together before the end of 1996 to decide whether a majority of countries were ready to adopt the single currency and whether monetary union could proceed. If a qualified majority of the member states supported these proposals, then they must set a date for monetary union of no later than 1 January 1999. Countries that join the single currency will have to confirm their participation by 1 July 1998. Following this confirmation, the executive board of the European Central Bank will be appointed and the value of the Euro will be set 'irrevocably'.

A further protocol set out the United Kingdom's reservations. It stated that the UK did not intend to move to full economic and monetary union unless it notified the European Council before the start of 1998, although provision existed in the protocol for the UK to change its mind. In the meantime, the protocol added, the UK excluded itself from the European central banking system and would have no voting rights in matters concerning it.

Maastricht set goals, mechanisms and timetables. At the time of writing, these remain in place, just as they were agreed at the start of the decade. But the context in which the treaty is being implemented is very different from the one in which it was drafted and agreed. The certainty and the optimism of 1991 – however confused they may have been – were palpable. Little of that remains today in any major nation of the EU. Of course nations that are unquestionable political and economic beneficiaries, such as Ireland, the Benelux countries, Finland, Portugal and Greece, continue to be enthusiasts for the treaty that they signed at Maastricht, although others (Denmark in particular) are more uncertain. But in all the major nations of Europe – Germany, France, Britain, Italy and, to an extent, Spain – the treaty has undoubtedly become an immense burden. The responses in these countries are, of course, distinct and national. But the fact that such nations are bearing the brunt of the disruption caused by the treaty underlines the radical nature of the project on which Europe is still embarked.

No European nation expresses the resultant anxieties more vociferously than Britain. Our people are deeply divided and uncertain about European monetary union and about Britain's engagement in the wider Europeanisation project.

This is nothing new. The argument has ranged across parties and within them. Britain's two main political parties have each radically changed their positions on Europe several times since the Second World War. For much of the period up to 1979, the Conservatives were the pro-European party. A majority of Conservatives followed Winston Churchill's instinctive postwar support for British involvement in European unification. It was the Conservatives under Harold Macmillan who first applied to join the European Economic Community in 1962. It was the Conservatives under Edward Heath who took Britain in ten years later. Though there were always 'anti-marketeers' in the Conservative ranks, many of them motivated by a nostalgia for empire which has all but disappeared today, the antis were a minority. Margaret Thatcher herself was an enthusiastic signatory of the Single Market reforms in 1986 which, in some readings, made the single currency inevitable. The idea that the Conservatives are the anti-European party in British politics is very recent.

As also is the idea that Labour is the pro-European party. It certainly was not that in the 1960s, when Macmillan began serious negotiations for British entry. Hugh Gaitskell famously told the 1962 Labour conference that British entry would mean the end of a thousand years of history. His successor Harold Wilson was cautious and undogmatic over Europe; he believed the arguments were finely balanced and was more concerned to ensure that the issue did not split his party, as in the end it very nearly did. Under Wilson, Europe became one of the talismanic issues for the rival Labour camps; the Left was bitterly opposed, while the Right was enthusiastically in favour and each side campaigned against the other in the referendum of 1975, which Wilson had authorised as the only way to avoid a complete split. Yet when the split did come, in 1981, Europe was one of the key issues in the formation of the Social Democratic Party and as late as 1983, Labour still campaigned for outright withdrawal. Under the leadership of Neil Kinnock, himself formerly a passionate 'anti-marketeer', Labour then began to move steadily in a pro-European direction, a direction which was continued under John Smith, a veteran pro-European, and up to the present under the more pragmatic leadership of Tony Blair.

For many in Britain, whatever party they support, the single currency argument is inseparable from a passionately felt argument about British history and identity, in which the sense of British independence is powerfully and offensively challenged by any attempt to assert that Britain's interests lie in a union with other European nations, especially Germany. Others believe, again irrespective of party and with no less certainty, that these deep instincts are nothing less than a historic illusion. They believe that this vision of a free-standing Britain has been irrevocably shattered by the collapse of the British empire, by the unavailing struggle to claim superpower status in a world manifestly dominated by the United States, by the rise of the Asian-Pacific powers and, not least, by the destruction of the British industrial base.

These potent instincts and passions surge through the debate about the single currency, sometimes blinding the participants to the sharper policy issues that are involved, but always acting as a reminder that what is at stake is much more extensive than a mere choice between economic alternatives.

We now turn to three distinctly different views about what Britain should do. First, the *Guardian*'s European Editor, John Palmer, an unrivalled Brussels-based observer of the evolution of the EU, argues the case for Britain's participation in the single currency. He is followed by the paper's

13

Economics Editor, Larry Elliott, who has been the *Guardian*'s leading voice in arguing against British participation in monetary union. Finally, the *Guardian*'s economics columnist and leader writer, Victor Keegan, puts the case for calculated caution, recognising the strength of the case for currency union, but emphasising the dangers of making the wrong move at the wrong time.

THE CASE FOR JOINING
JOHN PALMER

IN AN ERA of sweeping economic globalisation, European monetary union will provide an essential foundation for stable and sustainable growth that generates jobs. A single European currency will weaken the power of those who thrive on monetary chaos and financial speculation. It can also help ensure that the overweaning power of the global market place is better balanced and constrained by democratically decided economic and social priorities.

The mere ambition of the EU member states to aim for a single currency underlines the interdependence of the modern European economies, particularly since the launch of the single European market a decade ago. But European integration is itself, in part, a reflection of a global revolution, which has swept away many other national barriers concerning trade, finance, communication and investment.

This revolution has transformed the environment within which governments take decisions on growth, inflation and employment. It has eroded their power to influence economic outcomes. By requiring national states to share more of their economic 'sovereignty', European monetary union can, I believe, restore to EU governments collectively greater influence over economic developments than they can ever exercise alone.

No sensible calculation of the economic benefits of monetary union is possible without appreciating the costs of failing to adopt the Euro. If economic prosperity and fuller employment could be achieved simply by running large government budget deficits and by ignoring how they are to be financed, then the countries of the EU would have achieved economic nirvana long ago. But mounting government deficits and indebtedness throughout the 1980s and early 1990s produced, at best, spluttering economic growth, punctuated by deeper and more destructive recessions, declining global competitiveness and appalling levels of unemployment.

Too many on the British Left still share with the Eurosceptic right wing the delusion that currency devaluation offers a way out. But the British experience shows that devaluation – a move explicitly designed to cut real wages – simply does not work. Instead, it has helped to lock the UK into a cycle of low growth, low investment and low living standards. It has also entrenched 'short-termist' attitudes by British business at the cost of essential long-term, strategic investment.

In today's capitalism of 'real-time' global financial markets, countries that are thought to be running excessive budget deficits will get them financed only on onerous, and possibly ruinous, terms. The persistence of relatively high real interest rates (that is rates calculated after allowing for inflation) helps to explain continuing mass unemployment. Having to pay for nearly twenty million unemployed in the EU has thrown all government finances into crisis and has led to cuts in other essential public services.

There might be a practical alternative to monetary union if the clock could be turned back a decade or more to an era before global markets and global capital liberalisation. But apart from isolationist anarchies and dictatorships such a reversion is neither a possible nor desirable option for democracies. By reducing the disruptive powers of the financial markets, European monetary union can help governments begin to regain some control over global economic developments.

I do not see European monetary union as an end in itself. The logical next step ought to be for the EU to negotiate with the rest of the international community a more stable world monetary order. Together with the introduction of new global development goals, as well as new labour and environmental standards in the World Trade Organisation, the basis could then be laid for a trans-national politics, which is able to relate to global market forces from a standpoint of greater equality.

An expanding zone of monetary stability in the EU will create space to generate employment and other socially useful economic initiatives at regional and national levels. Supported by EU budget transfers and by a more vigorous European-wide investment-led recovery strategy, this is how national and regional economic adjustment within a monetary union is best assured.

The Hungarian financier George Soros, who reportedly made a multibillion-dollar fortune speculating in the currency markets in the early 1990s – notoriously speculating against sterling in the run-up to the ERM crisis – is an eloquent advocate of monetary union. He believes that it would be 'crazy' for the EU countries to reject a single currency and allow their economic fortunes to be decided by speculators. Soros says that 'a single currency is essential if the single European market is to be preserved'.

In summary, European monetary union will:

- lay the basis for long-term lower interest rates;
- encourage more investment and trade, by reducing instability and currency turmoil;
- reverse economic short-termism and create the foundations for sustainable growth and job creation;
- cut financial transaction costs (which are perhaps equal to 0.4 per cent of the EU's GDP), by eliminating the need for currency transactions or 'hedging' operations, where companies try to protect themselves against sudden currency fluctuations and, as a consequence, help to bring them about;
- create the conditions in which more efficient decisions can be taken in the allocation of economic resources.

These, then, are the advantages. But how do we get from here to there? To participate in the move to a single currency, countries have to meet the conditions set out in the Maastricht Treaty. It is true that these convergence criteria *could* be applied in a crudely deflationary fashion by EU governments when they decide, early in 1998, who qualifies to join the move to a single currency in 1999. But this would be profoundly counter-productive, because a narrowly dogmatic interpretation would make monetary union impossible. The consequent financial upheavals might even tear apart the European single market. The door would thus be opened to creeping national economic protectionism and to the political fragmentation of the EU itself.

A further misreading of the treaty's provisions for monetary union has led to alarmist predictions that Britain would have to make public spending cuts on such a scale as effectively to abolish the welfare state. In this context, a clear distinction should be made between targets for public spending and those for government budget deficits. Deficits are the consequence of spending exceeding all forms of revenue, including taxation. Indeed, those countries that have been most successful in curbing excessive deficits run higher levels of public spending than countries burdened with large deficits. Denmark, for example, which has virtually eliminated its budget deficit, has maintained high levels of public spending and has cut unemployment.

This needs to be emphasised because, listening to the critics, you would not be aware that after monetary union national governments will remain solely responsible for deciding how best to ensure that the deficit targets are met. This is where the genuine political battle about public spending and tax policies should be joined. Why do left-wing opponents of European monetary union simply echo those on the Right who say that deficits can be cut only by reducing social spending? There is no inevitability about this. Why not focus on other areas of spending – on arms expenditure, for instance? Above all, why do Labour critics of the single currency not campaign *for* higher taxes on capital and on the better-off, rather than mutely accept that monetary union means welfare cuts?

There is a lot of romantic self-delusion about the kind of alternatives favoured by these critics. Outside the single

18

currency, a Labour government would still be forced by the pressure of the international financial markets to keep the financing of deficits to 'acceptable' levels. The experience of past Labour governments suggests that hostile financial markets would impose much harsher terms for financing excessive deficits than those involved in qualifying for the single currency.

In the longer run, EU countries may want to run small deficits or even seek a broad budget balance. This is primarily to help finance the future social, pension, health and other needs of demographically aging European societies. But sustainable economic growth, by helping to reduce unemployment, will free up public-sector resources for other socially desirable purposes.

Monetary union is less an end in itself than a means to other economic ends. There is an unresolved debate about its wider and long-term economic goals. It increasingly embraces ideas such as a common tax policy (including possible EU 'green' taxes), new job-creating social market initiatives, and decisions about the scale of future wealth redistribution between the economically weaker regions of the EU.

Critics of monetary union should not insist on always assuming the worst, and should not be allowed to get away with this, either. No one can yet be certain how the Maastricht Treaty qualifying criteria will finally be interpreted when the decision is taken, by EU heads of government in 1998, on which countries will be allowed to move to European monetary union. Few of the fifteen EU countries as yet meet all the criteria – notably the treaty bench-marks for budgets deficits and government debt. But EU finance ministers pointed out in Verona in early 1996 that the Maastricht Treaty may allow higher deficits than the 3 per cent norm if they are seen to be both 'temporary' and 'exceptional' and if they are 'close to the reference values' set out in the treaty. The important thing is that EU heads of government should 'take into account' the overall performance of countries towards enduring economic convergence.

This flexibility has been criticised as fiddling the figures. In fact, it makes sense. Although average EU budget deficits have fallen from 6.2 per cent of GDP to only 4.5 per cent in 1996, inflation has fallen from an average of 4.1 per cent three years ago to just 2.5 per cent in 1996. No one doubts that inflation is under control. The treaty rightly provides enough leeway to ensure that there is little risk of excessive deflation in the run-up to monetary union in 1999. Indeed, as (admittedly opaque) references in the treaty to the 'golden rule' on public expenditure imply, it may even permit the bolder use of public spending than is generally appreciated, if this is strictly for investment, rather than consumption.

At the time of writing, the financial markets still believe that European monetary union will begin in January 1999 – just as foreseen in the Maastricht Treaty – and that enough countries will join to make the process credible. This timetable could still be disrupted if the current economic recovery is aborted and key candidates – notably France – fall too far short of the deficit target. But the determination of most EU leaders to meet the 1999 deadline should not be underestimated. This determination was further underlined by the agreement at the Dublin EU summit on a long-term stability pact, binding single currency countries to maintain financial disciplines after the start of EMU, at pain of substantial fines. Moreover, the popular credibility of the single currency has been strengthened by the publication of the proposed Euro notes in December 1996. No one has yet established how many countries are required to start monetary union, but the best estimate is that between six and nine countries will qualify in 1998, including the two essential players, Germany and France. Almost all the fifteen present EU members expect to be part of the Euro bloc by 2002, as do Malta, Cyprus and even some of the central European states now preparing for EU membership.

So the single currency is very nearly a fact, not just a possibility. Preparations are far more advanced than many in Britain like to realise. There is therefore a pragmatic case – as well as, in my view, a case based on principle – for examining the potential advantages for Britain if, and when, it goes ahead. Evidence submitted in 1995 to the House of Commons select committee on monetary union revealed some of these advantages. They include the contribution of the single currency to completion of the single European market – by far the most important destination for UK exports. But there are other advantages, too. Participation in the single currency would help insulate the United Kingdom from a repetition of monetary turbulence and would thus improve Britain's long-term economic under-performance. Britain's attractiveness as a site for international investment would be enhanced. Conversely, self-exclusion from the single currency could choke off important foreign investment in the UK.

We are not significantly more vulnerable to oil-price shocks, or more sensitive to movements in short-term interest rates, than other EU economies. Oil production currently accounts for only 1.85 per cent of our GDP. The Chancellor of the Exchequer, Kenneth Clark, has told the House of Commons, 'If it were the case that the British economy was so much more responsive to changes in short-term interest rates, I cannot understand why the devil we have had to move short-term interest rates around to the fantastic extent we have in recent years.'

Nor is there much substance to the view that Britain cannot join the single currency because sterling remains overvalued. The market view seems overwhelmingly to be that, measured against the United Kingdom's international competitiveness, sterling's current exchange rates are broadly appropriate. But the final rate at which sterling would join monetary union is open for the government to negotiate with its EU partners.

The goal of economic convergence should not be misunderstood. As the Shadow Chancellor, Gordon Brown, pointed out in Bonn in the summer of 1996, 'Real economic convergence does not mean that we have to have exactly the same levels of output or productivity. What is important is that their trend must not threaten to diverge faster than other means of adjustment . . . So it is a rounded judgement of the extent of real convergence and integration which we must make in deciding whether Britain can join, not just a mechanistic application of numbers.'

The problems facing the United Kingdom outside the single currency would be made worse if the British government were judged to be trying to wreck the entire monetary union operation by challenging its credibility. As the House of Commons EMU select committee was told by the City investment bank, Salomon Brothers, 'If the UK makes a judgement on the basis of the economic policies of our partners and publicly states our belief that we expect them to fail, then such a clear and strong vote of no confidence may well cause some friction with those partners. That could sour political and economic relations in a number of ways and would certainly put owners of British assets – both real and financial – on notice that there was an added risk in British policy.'

The City of London must expect to experience some disadvantages in the new single-currency system if the United Kingdom decides to remain outside. While overt discrimination against the UK by participating states is unlikely, the Governor of the Bank of England, Eddie George, has warned that 'the financial markets would penalise us – because they would be suspicious that we had stayed out because we did not feel that we could live with the disciplines.' In other words, it is a myth that the City is too strong to suffer from non-participation.

This brings me to an absolutely critical point. Whatever the British government's eventual decision, the opponents of a single currency have not sketched out even the outlines of an alternative economic and financial policy designed to deal with the consequences of unhitching the United Kingdom from a core project of all the other EU countries. Nor have they said what Britain should do in these circumstances to keep the 'confidence' of the international money markets.

Eurosceptics try to frighten voters by claiming that after monetary union all key economic decisions would be taken by an unaccountable European Central Bank, solely responsible for monetary policy. But how shocking is this in reality? In some EU countries, including Germany, the notion of central bank autonomy has strong political and trade-union support.

At present, European monetary policy is anyway largely determined, unilaterally, by the German Bundesbank – with precious little regard for anyone else's interests. If Britain adopts the Euro, this will change. Britain will have a seat on the board of the European Central Bank and a vote in all its decisions. It has no such representation on the councils of the all-powerful Bundesbank. Sole responsibility for macro-economic policy – including tax, employment and public spending – will remain with EU member states, acting both collectively and individually. Demonisation of the European Central Bank merely diverts attention from the real issue of the collective economic policies that we wish our governments to pursue together in a future monetary union.

I do not dispute that there is a case for strengthening the accountability of the new European Central Bank, particularly to the European parliament. The EU budget should also be increased to help economically weaker regions, although it is worth stressing that some 'peripheral' countries (such as Ireland, Portugal and Spain) have already made dramatic progress towards economic convergence. The EU should move to a common policy on some key taxes (including ecological taxes), partly to ensure that too much weight is not put on the purely monetary pillar of a single currency.

I also believe that much more could, and should, be done as part of the process to combat unemployment. It is true that all supporters of monetary union do not concur on what form of concrete action the EU should take to stimulate faster growth and more employment. Some ardent advocates of a single currency, such as Ken Coates, a Labour member of the European parliament, have proposed a massive increase in the borrowing powers of the European Investment Fund to help boost infrastructure and other job-generating investment. Others call for taxes on excessive corporate profits to help finance jobs in the socially useful and voluntary sectors, including the caring services and environmental protection.

EU governments can certainly be criticised for their collective failure to implement fully the growth and employment strategy set out by Jacques Delors nearly five years ago. But there is no evidence that abandoning monetary union will help to generate lasting jobs – quite the contrary. We can be sure that Britain will exercise precious little influence on these debates if it decides against the single currency even before 1998.

There is too much wishful thinking in Britain. British Eurosceptics cannot count on opposition from Germany or other EU countries to derail the entire process of monetary union. German public opinion, aware that the danger of unemployment due to an overvalued Deutschmark is far greater than any notional threat of Euro-generated inflation, is far less hostile now to the single currency. Nor can the United Kingdom expect to find allies even among those countries that may not be judged ready to join the move to a single currency in 1999. The Italian and Spanish governments accept that in their case entry to European monetary union may have to wait for a year or two. But, unlike the British, they regard themselves not as 'outs' but as 'pre-ins' preparing for early participation by joining a refurbished European exchange-rate mechanism. The Irish finance minister, Ruairi Quinn, has said that Ireland will join, even if Britain stays outside. The Finns expect to join by 1999 and the Swedes not long after. Even the Eurosceptic Danes will qualify and will then put the entire single-currency issue to a referendum.

Monetary union is possible without a parallel move to political union. But, unlike the increasingly xenophobic British Tory Eurosceptics, those who want to ensure that monetary union is harnessed to the goals of growth, jobs and social equity have every interest in supporting the democratic strengthening of the EU's institutions; in reducing the paralysing and reactionary bias of the national veto; and in moving to a decentralised European political union. At present this is better understood in Scotland, Wales and some of the English regions than it is by the political élite in London.

A British decision both to stay outside monetary union and to oppose any further move to political union in the Maastricht Treaty review conference could trigger a full-scale crisis in its relations with the EU. Some right wing Tory opponents of a single currency have already canvassed the idea of Britain renegotiating the overall terms of UK membership of the European Union. In such a confrontation, I believe that Britain would inevitably face further, and enfeebling economic, social and political isolation.

24

THE CASE FOR STAYING OUT

LARRY ELLIOTT

TWENTY-THREE YEARS ago, on the last occasion it won an election, Labour had no doubts about where it stood on the question of a single currency. Unlike the equivocating of the party's front bench today, Labour's 1973 Manifesto could not have been more explicit: 'We would reject any kind of international agreement which compelled us to accept increased unemployment for the sake of maintaining a fixed parity, as is required by current proposals for economic and monetary union.'

Labour's views on Europe may have shifted over the past two decades, but the argument that it originally deployed in opposition to a single currency is, if anything, even more powerful today than it was then.

Those in the United Kingdom who argue against monetary union are, then as now, a somewhat unlikely alliance of left-wing Labour MPs and right-wing Conservatives. Historically, though, there is an encouraging precedent for this *ad hoc* alliance: a similar coalition put paid to Harold Wilson's proposed reform of the House of Lords in 1969.

For some, the opposition to a single currency comes down to politics. On the Right, monetary union is a matter of sovereignty – a 'Who governs Britain?' question. On the Left, there is opposition to the idea that monetary policy should be conducted by a cabal of bankers, who by the very nature of their job tend to be conservative in their outlook, putting control of inflation above growth and jobs. These are important issues. Monetary union is rotten politics. But the reason it is rotten politics is that it is rotten economics.

Let's start with some statistics. In 1973, the final year of the long postwar boom, there were 3,712,000 people on the dole in the countries that make up the EU. By 1995 this total was exceeded by the unemployed in just one country, Germany. At the end of 1995 the jobless figure for the EU was an estimated eighteen million – and rising. In 1973 Europe's jobless rate was half that of the United States; today it is twice as high.

Enthusiasts for monetary union say that a single currency will be good for jobs and prosperity, and that it is needed to make the single market work properly. They are wrong. Moving to irrevocably fixed exchange rates will intensify the deflationary bias in European economic politics witnessed for the past twenty years, adding to unemployment and ultimately threatening to tear the EU asunder.

This is because political calculations, not hard economic imperatives, lie at the heart of the single-currency project. As Lord Lawson put it, when giving evidence to the parliamentary Treasury select committee in 1996, monetary union is being driven by Germany's fear of its past and by the French desire to 'corral Germany and abolish the Bundesbank'.

Explaining his objections to monetary union, the former Chancellor added, 'I don't want us to join because it's, at best, premature and, at worst, extremely damaging. It is likely to be damaging while the peoples of Europe are not in favour of submerging their autonomy, sovereignty and loyalty into a wider European loyalty. To do it prematurely would be to strain the political fabric and give full rein to xenophobes and demagogues in every country in Europe.'

As Chancellor, Lawson was wrong about many things, but about a single currency he was absolutely right. There is no popular support among the various peoples of Europe for submerging their separate identities to the European state-nation currently being planned for them by the élites in Brussels, Paris and Bonn.

Lawson's argument is worth following through. He went on to state that the two main advantages claimed for a single currency – no transaction costs for changing currencies within Europe and the elimination of exchange-rate uncertainty – were far outweighed by the economic drawbacks: 'The main disadvantage of a single monetary policy is that the larger, more varied and disparate the union, the less likely it is that the monetary policy will be appropriate for all parts of the union at all times.'

Wise words. The lessons of 1992 and 1993 – when the exchange-rate mechanism first creaked and was then blown apart – have not been learned in the capitals of Europe. Or, if they were, they have been swiftly forgotten. Britain's departure from the ERM on 'Black Wednesday' was not the result of a dastardly plot hatched by some spivs in the City and by George Soros, but occurred because the economy was being crippled by an economic policy that simply did not add up. Britain needed lower interest rates and a cheaper pound, and once the decision was made to suspend ERM membership, it got both. Under a single currency, neither policy tool would be available, because interest rates would be set by the fifteen central bankers running the European Central Bank and exchange rates would be fixed for all time.

In theory, the Maastricht convergence criteria are designed to ensure that all participating countries are in similar shape on the fateful day when the single currency becomes legal tender. But there were similar reassurances when Britain joined the ERM in 1990. How do we know that the public-spending cuts that have inflamed French workers and put demonstrators on the streets of Germany and Italy will do anything more than add a few hundred thousand to Europe's dole queues? What if the rate at which currencies are locked is not appropriate? What happens if, as in the aftermath of German reunification, interest rates suitable to cool down one part of the EU are completely at odds with those parts that need reflationary policies?

It is not sufficient, in response to these queries, to say that all countries will have their say in a collective decision. One vote out of fifteen does not equate with the Chancellor of the Exchequer deciding the monetary policy that he deems right for the United Kingdom's circumstances at any one time.

27

Britain has been a lone voice in Brussels since 1973, and there is scant evidence that that will change under the single-currency regime. Monetary union is likely to lead to a call for further harmonisations of laws and customs, crowned by a single fiscal policy, which in turn will further undermine public support for membership of the EU and perhaps puts the future of even the single market at risk.

It is said, of course, that economic sovereignty is a red herring, because Britain signed away large chunks of her sovereignty when she joined the European Community (EC) in 1973, and a lot more when Mrs Thatcher signed the Single European Act in 1986. But those who make this point need then to explain how it was that in the months leading up to Black Wednesday, the need to keep interest rates at a level to defend sterling's ERM parity resulted in unemployment touching three million and record levels of bankruptcies and home repossessions, while the months immediately afterwards, when base rates were cut by four percentage points and the pound was devalued by 15 per cent, resulted in immediate economic recovery. France, by contrast, was determined to continue with the self-flagellation of the *franc fort* policy, even after being given some breathing space by the 1993 general ERM crisis, and the result has been economic stagnation, unemployment running at 12 per cent and an alarming increase in xenophobia. There is economic sovereignty: all that matters is the will to use it.

The attempt to argue that only by huddling together can the puny nations of western Europe defend themselves against the might of the international financial markets reveals the design flaw in the whole monetary union project. Inherent in the 'ever-closer union' envisaged by the founding fathers of the EC, the idea of monetary union was shaped by two forces – the Cold War and the inflation shock of the mid-1970s, which ended the West's long postwar boom. But events move on. The Cold War is over and the great tide of inflation has ebbed, with each wave in the past two decades slightly weaker than the previous one.

Across the world, the 'big is beautiful' models of economic and political life are breaking down. Just as in the years following the First World War, the old empires are splintering into small entities based on nationality, race or ethnic grouping. In addition, the relentless rise in unemployment in the West to thirty-four million – levels not seen since the 1930s – has made the need for reflationary economic policies more pressing.

Set against this, the EU has a blueprint that encapsulates all the drawbacks of a system that is rapidly becoming old-fashioned: monetary union is big; it is top-down, taking power away from elected politicians and handing it to unelected central bankers; it will set deflationary policies in concrete.

Furthermore, the European model of development is starting to fray around the edges. Anyone looking for dynamism, for innovation, for new thinking about the right role for their firm and for industrial policy, would not look in the Ruhr Valley or on the plains of Lombardy – as they might have done ten or twenty years ago – but in California's Silicon Valley, where the new breed of young American entrepreneurs have chiselled out innovative ways of sourcing, financing and developing products. Europe, by contrast, has started to turn in on itself more and more trade is being conducted within the borders of the EU, where the lack of competitiveness is less of a problem than it is in the rest of the world.

As the non-partisan Centre for Economics and Business Research put it, 'The single currency is probably not going to solve Europe's competitiveness problems. Some of Europe's problems reflect overvalued exchanged rates and the single currency, by taking control of the German currency away from the Bundesbank, may help a bit here (albeit at the risk of inflation). But a considerable part of Europe's problems result from our wanting to have standards of living and of welfare and of social services at much higher levels than the rest of the world without being prepared to work either hard enough or productively enough to pay for them, and a single currency cannot change that.'

Some supporters of the Euro agree that it is no miracle cure. But, they insist, the alternative to moving ever closer is that the EU grows ever weaker and eventually falls apart. No compelling evidence is ever produced as to why this should be, or why the risk of Europe falling apart as a result of a single currency is smaller than the risk of it falling apart without a single currency. This deterministic, quasi-Marxist approach to history has in any case looked less tenable since the collapse of Communism and the break-up of the Soviet Union.

The lesson that European politicians should draw from the post-Communist era is that nothing is inevitable. The lesson that economists should draw is that the fifteen nations that make up the EU do not constitute the right raw material for a single currency. Germany, Austria and perhaps the Benelux countries could form what, in the jargon of economists, is known as an 'optimal currency area'. But for the EU as a whole, fundamental differences in language, geography, history, culture, labour regulations and tax systems prevent the component parts of the union achieving the sort of harmonisation envisaged from European monetary union.

Parts of Europe are highly productive; others are not. As a country becomes relatively less competitive, it has a number of choices. It can put a squeeze on its economy in a bid to reduce its costs to the level of its more favoured neighbours, or it can let its currency take the strain. Under monetary union, the second option would be outlawed.

Malcolm Sawyer and Phillip Arestis, two sceptical economists, wrote in the *Guardian* in 1996, 'The declining competitiveness which cannot be offset by devaluation will lead to declining output, income and employment. There is then a danger of a vicious circle setting in, as declining income leads to falling investment, a reduction in employment and outward labour migration.'

A similar point was made by Peter Jay in a *New Statesman* review of the 1996 book by a leading supporter of the single currency, Christopher Johnson.* Jay took issue with Johnson's claim that 'currency devaluation, like patriotism,

---

* *In with the Euro, Out with the Pound*, Christopher Johnson, Penguin, £7.99.

may be the last refuge of a scoundrel rather than a glorious manifestation of national independence'. Jay stated that it was not as a glorious manifestation of national independence that a change to the exchange rate was thought to be needed, but as a safety valve to adjust competitiveness deficits and 'thus to give a chance of escaping from the cycle of trade deficits, capital outflow, high unemployment, fiscal pressure, low profitability, low investment and general depression that afflicts an uncompetitive economy or region'.

The importance of the exchange rate for managing the economy can be fully appreciated only when the alternative courses of action for coping with a loss of competitiveness are investigated. For example, how realistic is it to expect mass migrations of workers from one part of Europe to another in search of jobs? Given linguistic and cultural differences, what chance would Italian receptionists have of finding jobs in Danish offices, or British local government officers have of working in Portuguese town halls? The increasing service-sector domination of Europe's economy means that it will be harder – not easier – for workers to become assimilated, even assuming that they are welcomed with open arms by the host populations and their political masters (which assuredly they will not be).

There is yet one more problem. In America a single currency is workable not only because the US has a single language and a shared cultural identity (the famed melting pot), but because it has a system of fiscal transfers that shifts resources to poor parts of the union from rich states. But to do this adequately, the US has a federal tax base that amounts to around 25 per cent of the GDP, ten times the current level of the EU's budget.

The conclusion is that unless the EU is fully harmonised and totally economically convergent before monetary union, it will be able to accommodate the resulting variations in economic performance only by deflation, migration or a single fiscal policy. The options are unacceptable, unworkable – or both.

Even in the hypothetical scenario that the nirvana of fundamental economic convergence could be achieved, there

31

would still be the risk of asymmetric economic shocks hitting one part of the EU more than others. In the US, for example, the defence cuts that followed the end of the Cold War affected California disproportionately.

The United Kingdom is likely to be at odds with the rest of Europe because our economy does not move in step with those of other European countries and is structurally different. An oil-price shock, for example, would have different effects in the United Kingdom and the rest of Europe, because the UK is a significant oil producer and our economy is more service-orientated than that of most other European countries. Increases in European interest rates would be more damaging in the UK, where households and companies tend to have variable-rate debt. Mortgage debt accounts for two-thirds of household income in the UK, compared with less than a quarter in Germany. Monetary union could actually increase the policy shocks here, rather than be a factor for stability.

So what does Britain have to lose by not clambering aboard the Euro-juggernaut? There are, of course, the famed gains to be made from abolishing transaction costs, but this amounts to a tiny proportion of GDP and is in any case decreasing all the time, as businesses learn how to hedge on the currency markets and individuals make use of credit cards.

Then there is the claim that the markets will force Britain to pay a premium on its interest rates for the pleasure of remaining on the outside, looking in. This was an easier argument to make before Britain left the ERM, and depends in any case on the policies followed at any one time. If, for example, the lack of European competitiveness led to a depreciation of the Euro against the dollar and the yen – a quite plausible scenario – Britain could easily enjoy lower interest rates than the rest of the continent. There is, in any case, no iron law in these matters. When the Swiss decided not to join the European Economic Area, their franc rose on the foreign exchanges. It was a similar story when Norway decided not to join the EU.

Finally, there is the canard that the City of London would lose out if Britain gave monetary union the cold shoulder.

Privately, nobody at the Bank of England believes this is true, for the simple reason that the City's primacy in the European time zone is based on its light regulatory regime and on its record of financial innovation. Making London part of a generalised European framework would be good news for the markets: in this case the markets of Paris and Frankfurt.

The clincher for the single-currency enthusiasts is that Britain has suffered for being a 'Johnny-come-lately' in the past and should not risk bringing up the rear again. This is ludicrous. Just because Britain made the wrong decision at Messina nearly forty years ago does not mean that it would be a mistake to stay out of a single currency in 1999.

It is as if, out there on the tarmac, is a jet destined for an unknown location. The danger of not getting on board is that all the best seats in club class will be taken and that, when Britain does decide to take the plunge, there will only be seats in steerage left. On the other hand, the plane has been on the tarmac for some time now and, for all the attention of an army of engineers, the suspicion is that one of the engines is a bit dodgy. The question is: would you get on board? Well, would you?

THE CASE FOR WATCH
AND WAIT
VICTOR KEEGAN

BRITAIN'S RELATIONS WITH a single currency are constantly being presented as an either/or. Either get married. Or get divorced. Yet the obvious solution is pre-marital cohabitation.

The decision whether to enter into monetary matrimony with the rest of Europe – until death do us part – is the single biggest economic decision Britain has had to make this century. If Tony Blair has to take that decision, it could make all the difference between Labour becoming the natural choice of government and sinking without trace after one term. It is more crucial than going on to the Gold Standard, because of the essentially irreversible nature of the deal. Small wonder that there has been so much debate about it. But there should be much more – particularly in France and Germany, where the politicians are still dominating the argument.

Don't believe the proselytisers who argue either that staying out would be suicidal or that entry would beget economic nirvana. They simply do not know. It is all a question of balancing unknown risks. There is a chance – say, evens – that monetary union will not make much difference either way. There is a 25 per cent chance that it could prove utterly disastrous, triggering much deeper unemployment than would otherwise have been the case. And there is probably an equal 25 per cent chance that it would help to rid Britain of her endemic tendency to award herself higher wages than other countries.

In the past, this problem has been periodically solved (and in very recent years solved effectively) by adjusting the currency – devaluing – in order to restore lost competitiveness. Entry into a monetary union would remove the devaluation option, while not necessarily influencing the chain of events (high wages, low productivity, etc.) that creates the need to devalue from time to time. For this to happen, Britain would need to undergo a cultural change so that people – from the board room to the shop floor – realised that if we pay ourselves higher wage increases than Germany or France, we will have to purge the excess inflation out of our system through higher unemployment.

In these circumstances, why not stand on the sidelines and watch the other players (especially France and Germany), who are driven by a demonic political agenda – which we do not happen to have – to sew themselves together at almost any cost? We not only do not have their political agenda, we do not have their economic profiles, either. France and Germany are much more likely to succeed with monetary union (notwithstanding the recent increase in unemployment in both countries) than Britain, with her history of inflationary wage growth and her dowry of North Sea oil, which is so vulnerable to sudden, sharp rises or falls in price. It is sobering to ponder what would have happened if Britain had been part of a single European currency when oil prices exploded in the late 1970s.

Far better, surely, in today's circumstances for Britain to participate as much as possible in construction of the mechanism for European monetary union, while postponing entry until sure that we have got our own house in order and that the 'core' currencies of Europe can prove they can run a single currency that does not turn into a machine for generating excessive European unemployment, as current experience of the Franco-German fixed exchange-rate system suggests.

One vital point that hardly anyone takes on board is that once, as seems likely, France, Germany and their satellites adopt a single currency, Britain will become an accessory after the fact, whether we like it or not. If we do not go into the single currency, it will nevertheless come to us. Once a 'strong' currency in the form of the Euro starts circulating in Europe, and is perceived to hold its value more successfully than the money of non-participating countries, then the whole currency game changes.

Big corporations in the United Kingdom will immediately adopt the Euro as the main medium for their loans. Farmers and European civil servants will be paid in it, and millions of people going abroad will want to use it for its sheer convenience (and the removal of high transaction costs). Euro-denominated charge cards will be in demand, especially from people travelling or holidaying in Europe.

Banks, building societies and insurance companies are already planning to meet an unexpected demand from punters wanting to have their savings put into a 'safe' currency to preserve its value, especially against the devaluation-prone pound if Britain stays out of currency union.

Once people have a plastic card denominated in Euros – complete with deposit account – it is only a small step to the likes of Tesco accepting it as payment at supermarket checkouts. It is worth remembering that about 95 per cent of the money supply already exists in digital form (the 1s and 0s of computer code) in building society and bank deposits. Less than 5 per cent of the total money supply is actually in circulation as physical notes and coins in the economy. At the moment 'smart cards' cannot cope with small amounts of money at the point of sale. But banks are working very hard on this (through such inventions as the 'digital purse', a plastic card that you can load electronically with your own money and then spend on small items).

It will not be long before the demand for Euros converges with improvements in electronic currency, to make it possible for people to use the Euro freely in shops in Britain whether or not we enter monetary union. Over time, people may also want their mortgages denominated in the hard Euro to preserve value. Then they might want to be paid in Euros, so that they do not fall into the trap of having to repay a mortgage in a strengthening currency out of depreciating pounds. How long then before the first wage negotiations are conducted in Euros?

The emergence of the Euro as a kind of Trojan-horse currency would be greatly accelerated if, instead of joining immediately, the government were actively to encourage the Euro as a second, or parallel, currency. In this way, instead of the decision to join a common currency being taken by the government from above, it would be taken individually by the people below. The existence of a parallel currency, moreover, would be a strong discipline on the government's monetary policy, because too much monetary laxity would make the Euro more popular as an insurance against inflation and would thus pressurise the government towards a policy that maintained the value of the pound.

It is worth mentioning all this because it underlines the merits of a 'wait and see' policy as a constructive strategy, rather than a cop-out. It would familiarise people with the strengths and weaknesses of a common currency, while allowing Europe to establish its own track-record. People in Britain will find it easier to assess the virtues of converting completely to the Euro if they have had several years in which it has been in circulation as a parallel currency.

This is also a good way to minimise the risks attached to irrevocable commitment to both the 'in' and the 'out' positions. Make no mistake: both positions carry enormous risks. Either side may be right. Frankly, we do not yet know. Too much of the running at the moment is being made by economists with an almost religious belief in the certainty of their own presumptions. This argument will never be settled by economic equations, because the outcome will be determined by millions of people exercising their own free will, whether as wage bargainers or as businesspeople, assessing the risks of investment. And the future will not necessarily repeat the past.

If monetary union delivered what its protagonists claim, and ushered in a period during which (as Christopher Johnson elegantly argues in his pro-EMU book*) interest rates were 1–1.5 per cent lower than otherwise, sterling crises

---

* *In with the Euro, Out with the Pound*, Christopher Johnson, Penguin, £7.99.

were banished, transaction costs between Europe's currencies eliminated, inflation reduced, pension funds better off and economic growth boosted by 0.5 per cent, then there would be no argument. We would all sign tomorrow.

Equally, there would be no argument if the fiercely anti-EU Bernard Connolly* is right in suggesting that monetary union will ultimately lead to political, as well as economic, ruin. The Germans, he argues, will agree to a European Central Bank only if the Bundesbank totally dominates it, as it has done the exchange-rate mechanism. For over a decade France has locked herself into a fixed exchange rate with the German Deutschmark in a vain attempt to control the Bundesbank, but it has never succeeded in getting interest rates down to German levels, despite very high unemployment of 12.5 per cent. France thus has all the burdens of monetary union without – so far – any of the benefits.

Britain's brush with fixed exchange rates (in the ERM) was even more bruising than the French experience until we extricated ourselves after Black Wednesday in September 1992. Since then the economy has enjoyed several years of growth which, although modest, has been greater than that of France and Germany and, in contrast to those countries, has ushered in a period of steadily falling unemployment.

If Britain had entered an irreversible monetary union rather than the exchange-rate mechanism then we would have been condemned to much higher unemployment (at least in the short term), resulting from British industry's inability to sell exports and compete at home with imports at an overvalued exchange rate. Euro-enthusiasts would argue that, even in this extreme case, the disadvantage to Britain would have been only temporary. This is because if we were locked into monetary union and deprived of the ability to adjust the 'nominal' exchange rate of the pound, Britain would be forced to change our 'real' exchange rate by improving competitiveness in other ways, including reducing labour costs through higher unemployment. This would be very

---

* *The Rotten Heart of Europe*, Bernard Connolly, Faber & Faber, £17.50.

messy and politically unpopular in the short term, but (it is argued) would not make much, or even any, difference in the long term.

Or would it? It is this difference between the short- and long-term effects of devaluation (and monetary policy) that lies – and certainly should lie – at the very heart of the debate. If devaluation merely makes good a short-term loss of competitiveness, which would be solved anyway inside monetary union (albeit at the cost of higher short-term unemployment), then the consequences of locking a currency into a permanent union would not be so great.

But suppose Britain kept on paying higher wages inside a monetary union, even though companies were forced to lay off workers (this is, after all, what happened during the 1980s)? Is there not then a danger that monetary union would become a permanent unemployment machine for the United Kingdom?

Some distinguished economists, such as William Buiter of Cambridge University, argue that changes in monetary policy (like raising or lowering interest rates), which Britain would give up in monetary union, do not actually affect long-term wealth creation. Monetary policy, Buiter argues, can do good or harm during transitional periods, but is not the stuff of which the wealth of nations is made. If this is true, then it not only undermines Connolly's arguments, but becomes a near-irresistible attraction to an incoming Labour government. Buiter contends that by closing the door on national monetary autonomy and throwing away the keys, Labour could save itself years of being tested by the international markets, without sacrificing long-term economic performance.

But is it really true that monetary policy is so irrelevant to long-term growth? Practically every economist now accepts that the 1979-81 recession in the United Kingdom – which destroyed up to 20 per cent of our industrial base – was the result of a sadistically severe monetary policy, in which interest rates were far too high. Surely the loss of so much industry – including many companies killed off by the lethal combination of an excessively overvalued exchange rate and high interest rates, which might have survived in calmer waters – must have had a significant long-term effect on the country's growth? What isn't there, cannot produce.

However, if we want to test the Buiter theory before committing ourselves to unknown dangers, let us indulge in constructive procrastination. Let us wait and see what happens to the French. They are already in the laboratory in the middle of a destruction-testing experiment. If, after ten years of economic purgatory directly caused by gluing the value of the franc to the Deutschmark, the French economy can resume its former growth path, then the benefits of the 'cold bath' arguments for intro European monetary union entry will be strengthened. But if France, with a much sounder long-term economic record than Britain (both in terms of economic growth and inflation), does not emerge victorious, would anyone place a serious bet on Britain doing better?

Membership of European monetary union is of course inextricably bound up with politics. Behind the entirely admirable aims of France and Germany to get closer together to avoid the possibility of future conflict – in which we all have a vested interest – lies a ruthless dash to achieve political and economic hegemony within monetary union. The Bundesbank is determined to maintain absolute control of monetary policy to guarantee the strength of the Deutschmark, while France is equally determined to break that hegemony, even if it costs unprecedented unemployment.

There are dazzling economic prizes to be won – especially price stability and lower interest rates – if monetary union succeeds, and unthinkable penalties if it does not. It is never going to work as easily as monetary union does in the United States, where there is much greater cultural and economic homogeneity than in Europe. This is another reason why Britain should wait until we are sure that our economy has 'converged' with France and Germany for a long period in key areas like inflation, exchange rates, budget deficits and unemployment (but not at current levels).

There is one specific area where we should wait to ensure that we do not converge: pensions. The rest of the EU has a truly huge overhang of unfunded pension liabilities. In France they are capitalised at 120 per cent of GDP (as against under

5 per cent for the United Kingdom). These unfunded liabilities could hold dangers (like higher interest rates) for taxpayers in other countries, including the UK, unless we are very careful. We should wait until we obtain reassurances before committing ourselves.

Europe could profitably use this period of waiting to improve its own common infrastructure (roads, railways and airlines) and to establish stronger European technology companies – including putting the Airbus consortium on to a proper commercial footing. Investment in a Europe-wide grid of optical fibres would do much more to improve the EU's competitiveness than espousing all the risks associated with a common currency. It could be argued – both logically and economically – that the establishment of a single currency should come at the end of a long process of welding Europe into a single market with a mutual infrastructure, rather than thrusting it on member countries when they are not really ready for it.

The worst mistake to make with regard to the single currency is the one that Britain made, when it entered the exchange-rate mechanism at a punitive rate: the assumption that membership of a harsh currency regime will somehow force companies and individuals to change their economic behaviour. It should be the other way round. Only when a country has changed its economic behaviour long enough to have established a decent track-record should it even contemplate locking itself into an (almost) irreversible regime.

That does not mean that we should get too hung up about surrendering economic power. The 'sovereignty' attached to conducting our own monetary policy is not worth having if someone else can do it better. If ceding powers to change interest rates to a single European Central Bank (on which we would of course have representation) could prevent a repeat of the gargantuan mistakes in monetary policy made in 1979-81 and in the late 1980s during the Lawson boom, it would be a small price to pay. It would also eliminate the propensity of governments to let the money supply rip during the run-up to a general election – though they could still manipulate fiscal policy. In *theory*, monetary stability and a stable currency ought to revive the ambitions of our corporations so that they could start investing again on a much bigger scale. In practice, alas, it does not happen that way, as can be seen in France, where over a decade of monetary stringency resulting from being tied to the Deutschmark has yet to produce the promised fruits. Why don't we sit this one out on the sidelines for a while?

A CONCLUSION

MARTIN KETTLE

NOBODY WHO HAS followed the preparations that have been taking place in Europe over the past year can be in any serious doubt that the single currency will now come into existence. It has rightly been dubbed 'a done deal' and much of the debate in Britain in recent months has consistently underestimated that fact. Our debates have been heavily impregnated with wishful thinking. We have imagined that the future of the single currency is more uncertain and contingent than in fact it is.

And yet, whatever the subjective certainties on the part of these who are promoting it, the wider European project of which the single currency is such a central part remains harder to predict than for many years. Beyond certain idealistic generalities, it is no longer obvious what Europe truly wants to be. It is certainly not the Europe that was formed by the Treaty of Rome, and which Britain joined in 1973. That Europe was a postwar solution in a Cold War context. The Maastricht Treaty was true to that tradition, even though the context in which it is now being implemented is radically different from the one in which it was conceived in the late 1980s. Postwar Europe has changed for good. Today, more than fifty years on from the last European war, the prospect of an inter-state European conflict seems incredible, even if one accepts that it cannot be purely theoretical. Europe now not only feeds itself but over-produces in agriculture on a stupendous scale. The idea of a political or military western European block as a 'third force' between the two Cold War superpowers is an anachronism.

And yet we remain the heirs to the agenda of those earlier times – common institutions, convergence of regulations, shared citizenship and, yes, the single currency – all of which made clear, if controversial, sense in that Cold War context. Today, in a new Europe, the boundaries and purposes of the EU are, to say the least, more unclear and historically problematic. They are certainly not properly defined in the minds of all Europeans. There is a compelling need to redefine the purposes and means of the European project afresh, in a post-Cold War Europe, giving the people of Europe an agenda that equips rather than encumbers them in these new circumstances. The rhetorical momentum that drove the old EU – the rhetoric of 'building Europe' and of 'ever-closer union' – is no longer adequate for the choices and decisions that face the people of Europe today.

If that is not done, there is a profound danger that the very institutions and projects that were originally conceived to bring Europe together will turn into their opposites and begin to force Europe apart. This is already happening in Britain, and there are signs that it is beginning to happen elsewhere, too. Taken to its most alarming extreme, it is possible to imagine a Europe in which the Treaty of Maastricht will come to be seen in some parts of Europe (perhaps even in Germany itself) as the Treaty of Versailles came to be seen in inter-war Europe – as the source of the problem, not the answer to it. If the attempt to satisfy the convergence conditions, or the effort to keep within the single-currency 'stability pact' is to cause (or even to appear to cause) the dismantling of the welfare and redistributive systems upon which millions of the poorest in Europe depend, then it could spark populist and nationalist backlashes in almost any state in the EU.

Yet it is fanciful to imagine that these anxieties are widely shared in the rest of Europe. Most members of the European political class believe that these are alarmist and improbable fears. Most member states of the EU have their own reasons for wanting to join the single currency, but there is broad agreement among them that it remains a desirable project, which must now go ahead and which it is far too late to stop.

For Germany, the most influential and powerful member state, this is a matter of high ideals; a means of ending conflict in Europe, of ensuring an era of unfolding peace between nations, and of anchoring and universalising the genuine benefits of sound German monetary policy for western, and ultimately eastern, Europe. For France, the second most important of the fifteen member states, monetary union remains – in spite of occasional qualms and considerable social disorder – the central political mechanism by which the power of Germany can be permanently corralled within a framework of European institutions.

For the other member states, individually unimportant by comparison with Germany and France, but all of them relevant players nevertheless, this is a project that they are determined to join, at almost any cost. This determination is sometimes seen in Britain as faintly absurd. Yet for some of the middle-ranking and small countries, and particularly for their technocratic élites, the creation of the single currency provides an almost unique opportunity to carry out policies that would otherwise be politically impossible. Italy is the most important example of this phenomenon. The single currency has give the Italian political class a chance to reorganise the terms upon which Italian society has for decades been run. In particular, it has offered an opportunity to restructure the labour market more flexibly, to disentangle Italy's complex network of state loans and holdings, and to break certain welfare commitments. Only external pressure from Europe could have brought this about. Italian popular support for the European project has enabled the country's institutions to take measures which, in earlier years, would have guaranteed governmental collapse, and which may yet do so anyway.

Others view the creation of the single currency less positively, but with just as much determination. For these nations, exclusion would be not just politically humiliating, but economically destabilising. The allure of the single currency for these nations is that it promises a monetary stability that they have rarely known, with budgetary discipline, low interest rates and controlled inflation creating a virtuous monetary circle which, they believe, will transform them. One may doubt the accuracy of this belief, even while acknowledging that it exists. These countries fear that such goals are unachievable outside the single currency, partly because they have not yet been achieved, and that failure to fulfil the convergence criteria and gain entry in the first wave in 1999 will send their finances into an uncontrolled spin, with social and political consequences at which they can only guess and which they certainly have no intention of experiencing. In short, they believe that they cannot afford *not* to join.

In Britain there is a tendency to look down on such reasoning. This attitude would be defensible if these various national processes were wholly unsupported by their nations' citizens, were being achieved by unacceptably coercive means, or were being achieved with flagrant dishonesty – or, indeed, all three. The British, and not only the Eurosceptic British, tend to assume rather too easily that many European governments are achieving convergence by fiddling the books and in the face of overwhelming public disquiet. It is undoubtedly true that there are examples of both, and also that they are significant phenomena in particular cases. But it is nevertheless a mistake to assume, as too many critics in Britain do, that *all* convergence to the Maastricht norms is being achieved disreputably and that *all* Europeans are fellow sceptics under the skin.

Like it or not – and the British Eurosceptics do not like it at all – most EU member states regard European monetary union and the single currency as decisions that were taken in the past and to which they are now bound, in honour, duty and self-interest. They took their decisions in various ways, about the adequacy of which one may reasonably argue, but they took them nevertheless. The Maastricht referendums in Ireland, Denmark and France are over. The parliamentary votes and constitutional court rulings in other member states have all been taken. That was the agenda of the early 1990s. The task for the late 1990s, they argue, is to make sure that the single currency has the best possible chance of succeeding.

It may at one stage have looked improbable that, even so,

it would work. Three events – the virtual collapse of the exchange-rate mechanism, the large public debts engendered by European recession, and the outbreak of serious trade-union resistance against attempts to meet the convergence criteria – combined to jeopardise the project in a number of countries, notably France, Italy and Spain. But during the late summer of 1996 that improbability began to recede rapidly from view. Talk of 'two speeds', first and second waves, core groups, and so on has become rarer and less serious than it was when it appeared likely that a majority of member states would have difficulty fulfilling the convergence criteria. Those who adopted the maximalist view, that monetary union was going to happen and that most member states would be part of it, have therefore been vindicated by events. In 1995, for example, only Luxemburg was able to keep within all the Maastricht criteria, while five member states (Greece, Italy, Portugal, Spain and Sweden) failed to keep within any of them. By the autumn of 1996 the European Commission was reporting a very different prospect. Its 1997 forecasts showed that France and Ireland were already under the wire, along with Luxemburg, with almost all other member states positioning themselves sufficiently close enough to the limits to have some serious prospect of qualifying. Only Greece remains entirely beyond the boundaries in all categories. The majority lie within sight of the line.

The extent of this convergence should not be under-estimated as freely as it is by British Eurosceptics. Nevertheless, it is true that significant and growing proportions of it are more apparent than real. The European Commission's statistics and assessments tend to underestimate the problems that a number of states are having. Take the example of government deficits. In 1996 eleven of the fifteen member states ran government deficits of more than the 3 per cent of GDP allowed under the terms of the Maastricht Treaty. Now – hey presto – in spite of rising unemployment and higher social costs, eight of the fifteen (including the United Kingdom) are predicting deficits of exactly, or about, 3 per cent for 1997, leaving only Italy and, more distantly, Greece outside the boundary. Technically, this means that all bar

Italy and Greece have therefore qualified on that count (and Italy is still busting a gut to squeeze its way in anyway). Yet the achievement is deeply unconvincing. To have so many member states qualifying both at the maximum allowable level and at the last possible moment is both disturbing and implausible for the future viability of the project.

We are watching the budgetary equivalent of crash-dieting. The nations of the EU are shedding economic flab by any means to hand, desperate to show that they can fulfil the slimming plan by the appointed day. When that day arrives, they may indeed discover to general acclaim that they tip the scales at the prescribed weight. Yet no one can seriously believe that the qualification is universally genuine, or that these late qualifiers have changed their ways for good. Binge (or sickness) beckons just around the corner. The notion expressed in the Maastricht Treaty that these achievements must be sustainable and consistent is not being put to the test; it is gradually being set to one side in the greater political cause of fulfilling the timetable. That is why so much depends upon whether Germany, as the chief dietician, is prepared to enforce the new slimline habits through the so-called 'stability pact' negotiated in the last weeks of 1996. Those who value the principles of truthfulness in public affairs must look to Germany to keep strictly to its word.

Yet the great fear remains that a blind eye is being turned too often, even in Germany. The crucial moment in this process was Germany's acquiescence in a manifest budgetary fiddle by France in autumn 1996. This allowed the French government to raid the coffers of France Telecom to enable it to squeeze the deficit to meet the qualifying criterion. Having allowed its ally France to cheat, Germany and the other European nations were then in a weak position to deny less favoured nations a similar creative largesse. Within weeks, Italy duly came up with a proposal to impose a repayable tax on its citizens in 1997, explicitly to enable the country to get under the wire with an acceptable deficit, even though the plan also envisaged returning this tax to the voters once Italy had qualified. The Italian plan, needless to say, was accepted. At this rate, it is clearly only a matter of time before the EU declares even a spectacularly unqualified and unconvergent country such as Greece to be a model of monetary rectitude like all the others. The only thing that is more certain is that Britain, by pursuing its lone disruptive role in Europe over so many matters for so long, has absolutely no influence upon any of these outcomes.

But Britain, like all the other nations – in or out – will have to face the consequences. What, in the end, should Britain do? The principle of a single currency operating in a single market, binding Britain more closely to an ever-enlarging Europe bound by an 'ever-closer union', is rightly an attractive one to many people. It appears to make sense of the British national journey in the twentieth century, a journey that has taken it steadily downwards from global imperial power, through junior nuclear superpower to gently declining, middle-rank, developed-country status. It could provide a guarantee of the low inflation and low interest-rate economy that any sane trading nation would like to achieve and sustain for the benefit of its people. It could remove at one swoop the exchange-rate nightmare that has plagued the country so often in the postwar era. For a prospective Labour government, the chance to be rid of the international currency-market crises that have beset every one of its predecessors is incredibly tempting, although deregulation of the currency markets has already done much to reduce the problem.

Joining the single currency would embody the belief of many people – including whole generations of policy-makers and large numbers of exporters – that Britain must accept that it is a European nation, or it is nothing. But the problem is not simply that there are such serious economic risks attached to a project that has been so peremptorily conceived and so disreputably implemented. The problem is essentially political. It is clear that Britain does not, and perhaps cannot, accept the proposition that it is yet – or perhaps ever will be – this kind of European nation. The opinion polls and the 1975 referendum consistently show that the British are willing members of a European Union. But nobody can seriously pretend that the British people are enthusiasts either for the single currency itself or for the kind of European Union that the single currency would almost inevitably portend.

Perhaps there might have been enthusiasm, if modern British political history had been played out in some other way. But might-have-beens are no basis for forward-looking politics. The Eurosceptics, flying the flag, pandering to nationalist feelings and enjoying a steady supply of ammunition courtesy of the Europhiles in Britain and elsewhere, have consistently carried the argument against the pragmatists. That does not make them right, but it does make them powerful. Even if they are a minority, they remain a strong enough minority to wreck the enthusiasts' dream, especially because the enthusiasts have been consistently complacent, and occasionally dishonest, about the eventual outcome of the policies that they espouse. To use an analogy that would undoubtedly appeal to many of them, the Eurosceptics are the Ulstermen of the Irish crisis of 1920-1. They have the power to prevent the implementation of the treaty. The Europhiles may not like them, but the Eurosceptics cannot be ignored and they will not go away.

In 1994 and 1995 there was a widespread view in other European capitals that the election of a Labour government would transform the nature of Britain's engagement with the European unification project. Continental Europeans, dismayed by the years of semi-detached confrontation with Conservative governments led by Margaret Thatcher and John Major, imagined that a Labour government led by John Smith or, later, by Tony Blair would be an altogether different partner. If the sole tests of that partnership were goodwill and a general willingness to think positively about the EU, then that assumption would have been proved right. But the more Europe got to know about the Blair Labour Party, the clearer it became that Labour was not willing to make the decisive institutional commitments that the continental European states wanted to see. Labour, they discovered, was constrained in many of the same ways that the Conservatives were. It may be true that Labour would not have handled the BSE crisis as obdurately as the Conservatives, and that Labour would revoke the United Kingdom's Maastricht opt-out on the so-called social chapter. But on the big institutional initiatives, that are integral to the unification project – the European parliament, the enhanced commission, majority voting, common foreign policy and, above all, the single currency – Labour was very nearly as cautious as the Conservatives.

This is because Euroscepticism is now sufficiently rampant in British political life to constrain the ambitions of any government, not just a Conservative one. To ask any British government to join the single currency is to ask it to sacrifice all of its other priorities in favour of this effort. In the event of deciding to join, all major British parties have now committed themselves to a constitutional process that will not only last a very long time, but which will also test the unity of party and government to the utmost. Quite properly for such an important issue, the Conservatives and Labour now support a referendum on the single currency, but a referendum that would take place only after the Cabinet had voted in favour of entry and after legislation to enter had been passed by parliament. The political risks of such a course are pro-digious. They include not merely the problem of maintaining Cabinet and party unity on the issue, but that of getting the legislation through parliament. Behind all these traps lies the British tabloid press, gripped by anti-European feeling, sometimes xenophobic, and, in 1996, apparently happy to go to war over a football match, let alone the future of the pound. This all adds up to a formidable enough set of dis-incentives for any government, let alone one that is divided over the issue and uncertain about the benefits, as any British government in this position is likely to be.

To ask a Labour government, coming to power in 1997 for the first time in nearly two decades, to submit itself to this process is surely a particularly exquisite form of torture. Can anyone who has longed for the defeat of the Conservatives seriously want a Labour government to hurl itself on the rocks over the single currency, before it has even had time to carry out any other substantive business? It is a farcical proposition. If there were one issue that would reunite a defeated and demoralised Conservative Party, it would be the prospect of wrapping itself in the Union Jack and attacking Labour as the traitors' party. A Labour government that tried to enter the single currency would be politically overwhelmed.

To oppose British entry into the European single currency is not to oppose Europe, or even to oppose the principle that a single currency may be desirable. But it is to say that *this* European single currency is flawed and potentially dangerous and that Britain would be better served staying out of it for the time being. Our interests are better advanced by watching supportively from the sidelines than by attempting to commit a sceptical British public to such a project at such a time. If we believe that the single currency is worth joining then we must set about the task of persuading public opinion and winning the argument. This cannot be done in the timescale which would be necessary in order for Britain to join in the first wave, however desirable such a course might otherwise seem to pro-Europeans.

Economically and politically, it is not a risk worth taking in this country at this time. Even those who would like the single currency to succeed in the future ought to hope that it does not come about now. Much depends on Italy, by far the most important of the committed, implausible, first-wave 'wannabes'. If Italy fails to meet the Maastricht criteria, then a workable evolutionary single currency project, in which countries which are economically unprepared (like Italy) or politically unprepared (like Britain) may join another day in a second wave. One day, perhaps, the single currency may evolve as a natural and safe embodiment of Britain's troubled European identity. But not this single currency and not this country in its current mood. Not now. And probably not even in the next five years, either.

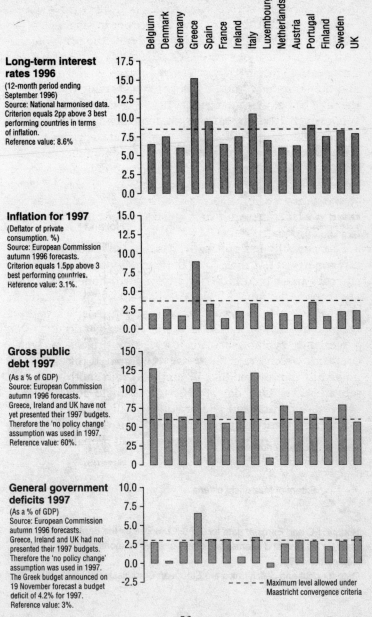

Long-term interest rates 1996

(12-month period ending September 1996)
Source: National harmonised data.
Criterion equals 2pp above 3 best performing countries in terms of inflation.
Reference value: 8.6%

Inflation for 1997

(Deflator of private consumption. %)
Source: European Commission autumn 1996 forecasts.
Criterion equals 1.5pp above 3 best performing countries.
Reference value: 3.1%.

Gross public debt 1997

(As a % of GDP)
Source: European Commission autumn 1996 forecasts.
Greece, Ireland and UK have not yet presented their 1997 budgets.
Therefore the 'no policy change' assumption was used in 1997.
Reference value: 60%.

General government deficits 1997

(As a % of GDP)
Source: European Commission autumn 1996 forecasts.
Greece, Ireland and UK had not presented their 1997 budgets.
Therefore the 'no policy change' assumption was used in 1997.
The Greek budget announced on 19 November forecast a budget deficit of 4.2% for 1997.
Reference value: 3%.

- - - - - Maximum level allowed under Maastricht convergence criteria

53

CURRENT PERFORMANCE RELATIVE TO THE MAASTRICHT CRITERIA

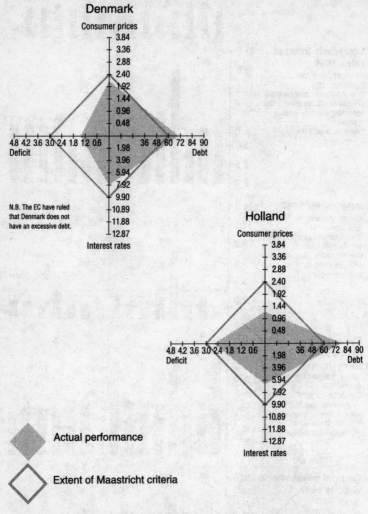

Denmark

Consumer prices

N.B. The EC have ruled that Denmark does not have an excessive debt.

Deficit

Debt

Interest rates

Holland

Consumer prices

Deficit

Debt

Interest rates

Actual performance

Extent of Maastricht criteria

Source: EC and Eurostat data for 1996. Compiled by the Bank of England.
Data for inflation and interest rates refer to a twelve month period ending
September 1996.
Data for debt and deficit ratios are European Commission autumn 1996
estimates.

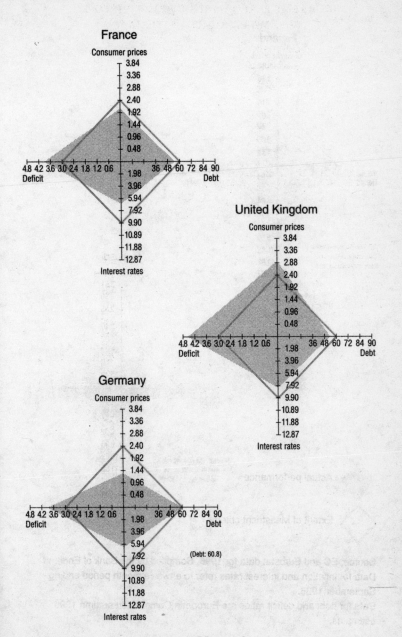

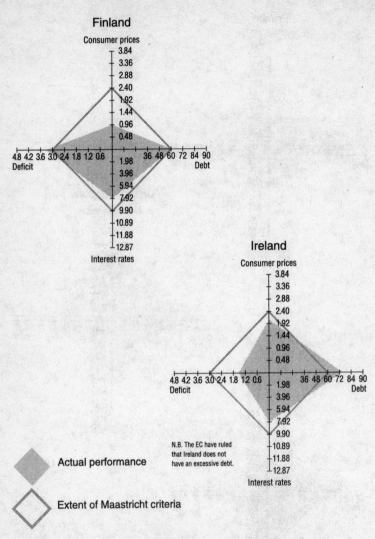

Finland

Ireland

N.B. The EC have ruled that Ireland does not have an excessive debt.

Actual performance

Extent of Maastricht criteria

Source: EC and Eurostat data for 1996. Compiled by the Bank of England. Data for inflation and interest rates refer to a twelve month period ending September 1996.
Data for debt and deficit ratios are European Commission autumn 1996 estimates.

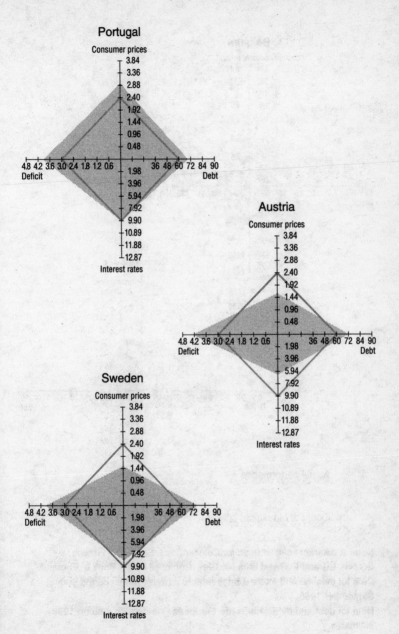

57

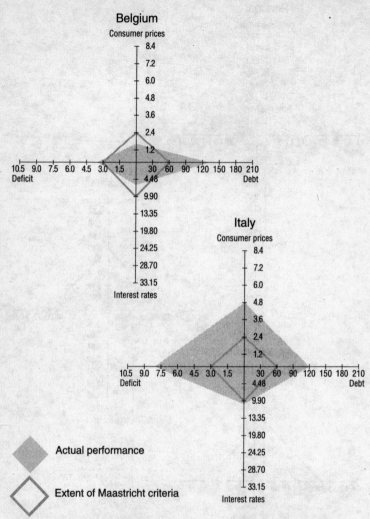

Belgium

Consumer prices

Deficit

Debt

Interest rates

Italy

Consumer prices

Deficit

Debt

Interest rates

Actual performance

Extent of Maastricht criteria

Note: A different scale is used for Belgium, Italy, Spain and Greece.
Source: EC and Eurostat data for 1996. Compiled by the Bank of England.
Data for inflation and interest rates refer to a twelve month period ending
September 1996.
Data for debt and deficit ratios are European Commission autumn 1996
estimates.

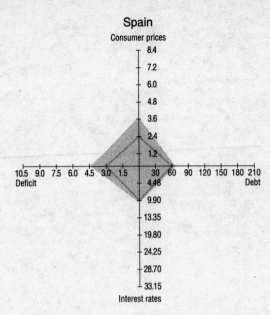

Spain

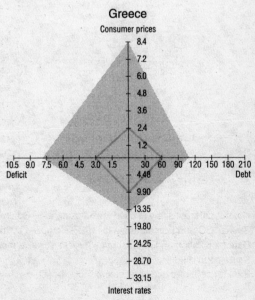

Greece

GLOSSARY

BLACK WEDNESDAY: Wednesday 16 September 1992 – the day when sterling was driven out of the EMU exchange rate mechanism; a defining day for John Major's 1992-97 premiership and for many Eurosceptics.

CONVERGENCE CRITERIA: Terms agreed at the Maastricht conference in 1991 under which European Union member states would bring their financial policies into line in order to be eligible to join the single currency in 1999.

EURO: Name agreed for the single European currency; in full circulation from 2002.

EUROPEAN CENTRAL BANK (ECB): Bank created under the Maastricht Treaty to issue and regulate the single currency from 1999; before then, the transitional banking institution is known as the European Monetary Institute. Both are based in Frankfurt.

EUROPEAN COMMISSION: Executive arm of the European Union, based in Brussels, currently chaired by Jacques Santer.

EUROPEAN COUNCIL: Decision making body of the European Union, normally comprising ministers from each member state government; changes its composition according to the subject under discussion (e.g. agriculture, finance, transport).

EUROPEAN ECONOMIC AREA (EEA): Established in 1993 to allow non-EU nations (such as Norway) and the EU to share free movement in goods, services and people without further political association.

EUROPEAN ECONOMIC COMMUNITY (EEC): Forerunner of the current European Union, established by the Treaty of Rome in 1957.

EUROPEAN INVESTMENT FUND: Financed by EU member states, it provides long-term loans or guarantees to promote European economic equalisation and integration.

EUROPEAN MONETARY SYSTEM (EMS): A voluntary system of fixed exchange rates between EU member states created in 1978; the precursor of EMU.

EUROPEAN MONETARY UNION (EMU): Three stage process agreed at Maastricht in 1991 in which the EU states create the single currency by 1999.

EUROPEAN UNION (EU) The association of member states originally set up under the Treaties of Rome and Maastricht, now greatly expanded in size and scope; currently contains 15 members (Britain joined in 1973).

EUROSCEPTIC: Term loosely applied to opponents of the Maastricht process and, in some but not all cases, of British membership of the European Union.

EXCHANGE RATE MECHANISM (ERM): Formal set of voluntary exchange rate relationships between EU member state currencies in which rates may not exceed specified bands; severely damaged in 1992-93 but recreated before completion of the single currency.

GROSS DOMESTIC PRODUCT (GDP): The total value of a country's output of goods and services over a specified period (normally a quarter or a year) regardless of ownership.

'INS'/'OUTS': Commonly used shorthand to differentiate those countries which will join the single currency and those which will not.

OPT-OUT: Sections in the Maastricht Treaty which allow named countries not to implement particular clauses which are otherwise obligatory; the UK has an opt-out over both the social chapter and the single currency.

SOCIAL CHAPTER: Section of the Maastricht Treaty dealing with employment rights.

STABILITY PACT: Agreement among EU member states for the maintenance of financial disciplines after the creation of the single currency; enforceable by fines.

TREATY OF MAASTRICHT: Treaty which sets out next stages of the EU's progress to monetary and political union. Signed at Maastricht in 1991.

TREATY OF ROME: Treaty which created the European Economic Community in 1957, setting the member states on a path towards 'ever closer union'.

WORLD TRADE ORGANISATION (WTO): International body established to promote global free-trade; set up in 1993 following the 'Uruguay Round' of negotiations under the General Agreement on Tariffs and Trades (GATT), which it supersedes.

EMU Chronology

10-11 December 1991: Maastricht Summit agrees to create a single currency in 1999

16 September 1992: Black Wednesday. Britain leaves exchange rate mechanism

4 Novembe 1992: Tory rebels stage first Maastricht rebellion

1 January 1993: Maastricht Treaty comes into force March 8, 1993: Tory rebels defeat Government on Maastricht Bill

20 May 1993: Maastricht Bill passed by Commons. 41 Tories rebel.

25 September 1993: Britain will not join single currency 'within the foreseeable future' – John Major

1 May 1994: Michael Portillo says Britain must 'never' agree to a single currency

28 November 1994: Conservative whip withdrawn from eight Euro rebels led by Bill Cash MP

24 April 1995: Whip restored to Tory Euro rebels

8 December 1995: Madrid Summit confirms 1999 as start of final move to monetary union and a single currency

19 January 1996: Government announces it will issue a White Paper on further European integration.

7 March 1996: Former Chancellor, Nigel Lawson, attacks Conservative Party plans on the single currency

29 March 1996: Turin summit begins inter-governmental conference to review the Maastricht Treaty

2 April 1996: Government promises to hold a referendum if a future Tory government decides to join a European single currency

10 April 1996: Millionaire businessman Sir James Goldsmith announces plan to run pro-referendum candidates against sitting MPs in the general election

24 April 1996: Bill Cash 'sovereignty' Bill to overrule European Court of Justice wins 66 Tory votes

22 September 1996: Clarke says it would be 'pathetic' if UK waited while other countries launched single currency

30 October 1996: Lord Healey warns convergence will produce 'riots on the streets'.

17 November 1996: Blair promises Labour will hold referendum on single currency

21 November 1996: Major refuses call for immediate single currency debate from Sir Marcus Fox of Tory backbench 1922 committee.

2 December 1996: Clarke says it would be 'preposterous' to reverse government policy of keeping options open.

14 December 1996: EU heads of government meet in Dublin to confirm the 1999 starting date of the single currency and agree details of the economic 'stability pact'.

THE EURO IN YOUR POCKET

What will the Euro mean to me . . . if Britain joins?

THE SINGLE CURRENCY won't make any physical difference to our lives for five years. Then, in 2002, it will be a bit like being hit by decimalisation and a changeover from fahrenheit to centigrade on the same day. People will not only have to cope with what the Euro in their pocket is worth but also whether traders are using the opportunity to put their prices up to recoup some of the cost of converting their machines and accounts systems to the new currency. The situation may be even more confusing because the new and old notes will be in parallel circulation for six months. Some experts think that it would be better to have a 'big bang' at the beginning – forcing everyone to come to terms with the new situation rather than having an extended period of dual currency. All our wages, loans and mortgages will be denominated in Euros and, to the extent that the Euro becomes a stronger currency than the pound, our savings will be less prone to be eroded by inflation.

In December 1996 the European Union revealed what the new Euro notes will look like, though they won't go into circulation until January 2002. There will be seven different notes varying in value from 5 Euros up to 500 Euros. Coins will follow later. The notes are of different colours with windows, bridges and doorways symbolising the opportunities of the new Europe. No final decision has been taken on how much a Euro will be worth but if the French preference for the Euro to have the same value as the Ecu (the existing artificial currency) wins through, then the Euro will be worth about 75p. Unlike the Euro – which will be a real currency whose circulation will be strictly controlled by the proposed European Central Bank – the Ecu (European Currency unit) is merely a device to back corporate and government debt. Its value is based on a 'basket' of currencies (including the French franc, the German mark and the British pound) and its value fluctuates daily according to the value of the currencies in the basket.

The most visible benefit of the new regime will be that we won't have to buy foreign currencies when going abroad on holiday or for business. It will also be easier to compare relative prices in different countries – and also wages. It could lead to some groups of workers like teachers asking for more money. The price of goods will still be different in other countries and in different parts of those countries (reflecting factors like local labour charges, transport costs or higher profits): but inflation in general ought to be lower because of the determination of the European Central Bank to contain inflation and to maintain a strong currency.

And what will it mean to me . . . if Britain does not join?

No one will have to use the Euro. The pound will remain the official currency. However, there will be nothing to stop anyone taking out a plastic credit card denominated in Euros for their foreign trips. Building societies and banks are preparing deposit accounts and assurance policies denominated in Euros to meet any demand there might be for people to hold their savings in a 'strong' currency accepted by most of the rest of Europe. Some stores, like Marks & Spencer, have already announced that their new tills will be converted to take Euros or pounds even if Britain does not join the single currency. In other words, if we join monetary union then the Euro will become compulsory; but if we do not it will be voluntary.

THE STATE OF THE NATION

*Vintage Books that tell you where we are,
how we got there and where we're going...*

Will Hutton

THE STATE WE'RE IN

The Number One Bestseller

On the hardback bestseller list for more than six months,
The State We're In is the most explosive analysis of British
society to have been published for over thirty years. It is now
updated for the paperback edition.

'His optimism is unquenchable, his excitement exhilarating
and his creativity awesome'
David Marquand, *Observer*

'Now, in Hutton's book, we have at last what we need – an
impassioned, and passionately cogent, critique of New
Right policy'
John Gray, *Guardian*

'If Will Hutton were a political party I would vote for him'
David Aaronovitch, *Independent*

VINTAGE

The Commission on Social Justice

SOCIAL JUSTICE

STRATEGIES FOR NATIONAL RENEWAL

'Essential reading for everyone who wants a new way forward for our country'
Tony Blair

The UK needs new direction. We need to be clear about our
values, understand the forces shaping change, create our
own vision of the future – and then set out to achieve it. Our
fate is not determined; we can bridge the gap between the
country we are and the country we would like to be. This
book shows how.

'John Smith's anger at the state of Britain today led him to
establish the Commission on Social Justice. Its report will
inform Labour's policy making and provide the basis for a
vital national debate about the future of work and welfare.
It is essential reading for everyone who wants a new way
forward for our country'
Tony Blair MP

VINTAGE

The Commission on Public Policy and British Business

PROMOTING PROSPERITY

A BUSINESS AGENDA FOR BRITAIN

'A stimulating report worthy of wide debate'
Sir Ronald Hampel, Chairman of ICI

Promoting Prosperity: A Business Agenda for Britain is the final report of the Commission on Public Policy and British Business in which senior business leaders and eminent academics call for a new relationship between government and corporate Britain.

After wide consultation with the business, policy-making and academic communities, the Commission identifies current failings and successes in UK economic performance and sets out a wholly different vision of public policy towards business. It argues that government should strike the right balance between promoting competition, encouraging cooperation and ensuring the supply of high quality inputs, to provide the right incentives and environment for private business to perform better.

Far reaching and challenging, *Promoting Prosperity* is certain to set the agenda for British business now and into the twenty-first century.

VINTAGE

David Rose

IN THE NAME OF THE LAW

THE COLLAPSE OF CRIMINAL JUSTICE

The book behind the BBC Television Series *The Verdict*

'A stunning critique of the criminal justice system...Rose brilliantly unravels the complex relationships and philosophies which sustain a system in crisis and calls for a radical rethink. While his proposals for reform may be controversial, they must also be taken seriously. We ignore his challenge at our peril'
Helena Kennedy QC

'Combining crime correspondent's reportage and academic analysis, Rose charts a devastating portrait of an ailing criminal justice system'
Kevin Toolis, *Observer*

'A work of meticulous honesty...Rose has triumphantly grasped and passionately presented the big issues in a decade of upheaval and change in the English system of fairness and justice'
John Stalker, *Sunday Times*

'Very thoughtful, well-documented and timely'
Ludovic Kennedy, *Daily Telegraph*

VINTAGE

Also available in Vintage

Ian Jack

BEFORE THE OIL RAN OUT

BRITAIN IN THE BRUTAL YEARS

'The finest feature writer in Britain'
Jeremy Paxman, *Independent*

Before the Oil Ran Out is a collection of articles that have
won Ian Jack well-deserved acclaim, including Granada
Television's Journalist of the Year Award for 'brilliant fea-
tures painstakingly researched and dazzlingly written with
the heart as well as the head'. An absorbing account of the
changing face of Britain, *Before the Oil Ran Out* is a timely
portrait of an increasingly divided nation.

'Jack's opportune pieces coalesce into a portrayal of a
British decade, witty, sometimes moving, always intelligent'
Daily Telegraph

'Full of good things: vastly enjoyable, funny, with the occasional flash of observation that illuminates experiences
many of us recognise but have never articulated'
New Society

'He belongs to a tradition that goes back to Cobbett and
even Defoe – and his sharp eyes, ears and wit make him well
worthy of it'
Financial Times

VINTAGE

THE STATE OF THE NATION
A SELECTED LIST OF VINTAGE BOOKS

☐ MANUFACTURING CONSENT	Noam Chomsky and Edward S. Herman	£8.99
☐ PROMOTING PROSPERITY	Commission on Public Policy and British Business	£8.99
☐ SOCIAL JUSTICE	Commission on Social Justice	£6.99
☐ BLOOD, CLASS AND NOSTALGIA	Christopher Hitchens	£7.99
☐ COMING BACK BROCKENS	Mark Hudson	£7.99
☐ THE STATE WE'RE IN	Will Hutton	£7.99
☐ BEFORE THE OIL RAN OUT	Ian Jack	£7.99
☐ THE SPECTRE OF CAPITALISM	William Keegan	£6.99
☐ EVE WAS FRAMED	Helena Kennedy	£7.99
☐ THE ENCHANTED GLASS	Tom Nairn	£6.99
☐ IN THE NAME OF THE LAW	David Rose	£7.99
☐ THE VINTAGE BOOK OF DISSENT	Edited by Michael Rosen and David Widgery	£8.99

- All Vintage books are available through mail order or from your local bookshop.
- Please send cheque/eurocheque/postal order (sterling only), Access, Visa or Mastercard:

☐☐☐☐☐☐☐☐☐☐☐☐☐☐☐☐

Expiry Date:_____Signature:_____

Please allow 75 pence per book for post and packing U.K.
Overseas customers please allow £1.00 per copy for post and packing.

ALL ORDERS TO:
Vintage Books, Book Service by Post, P.O.Box 29, Douglas, Isle of Man, IM99 1BQ.
Tel: 01624 675137 • Fax: 01624 670923

NAME:_____

ADDRESS:_____

_____

_____

Please allow 28 days for delivery. Please tick box if you do not
wish to receive any additional information   ☐
Prices and availability subject to change without notice.